Conversa

Italian

Dialogues

50 ITALIAN CONVERSATIONS TO EASILY IMPROVE YOUR VOCABULARY & BECOME FLUENT FASTER

CONVERSATIONAL ITALIAN DUAL LANGUAGE BOOKS VOL. 1

TOURI

https://touri.co/

ISBN: 978-1-953149-16-9

CONTENTS

WANT THE AUDIOBOOK FOR FREE?

We have a **limited** amount of **free** promotional codes for this audiobook.

Here's how it works:

1. **Visit the link below** to see the listing on AudiobookRocket
2. Request a free promo code from us
3. In **30 days** leave an honest, unbiased review on the audiobook.
4. Confirm & notify us on AudiobookRocket that you left a review.
5. Request and enjoy additional audiobooks from other publishers on the site.

https://audiobookrocket.com/audiobooks/20

IF YOU ENJOY THE FREE AUDIOBOOK,

PLEASE HELP US OUT AND **LEAVE A REVIEW**

RESOURCES

TOURI.CO

Some of the best ways to become fluent in a new language is through repetition, memorization and conversation. If you'd like to practice your newly learned vocabulary, Touri offers live fun and immersive 1-on-1 online language lessons with native instructors at nearly anytime of the day. For more information go to Touri.co now.

FACEBOOK GROUP
Learn Spanish - Touri Language Learning

Learn French - Touri Language Learning

YOUTUBE
Touri Language Learning Channel

ANDROID APP
Learn Spanish App for Beginners

BOOKS

Intermediate French Short Stories (Volume 1): 10 Amazing Short Tales to Learn French & Quickly Grow Your Vocabulary the Fun Way!

PORTUGUESE

Conversational Portuguese Dialogues: 50 Portuguese Conversations and Short Stories

ARABIC

Conversational Arabic Dialogues: 50 Arabic Conversations and Short Stories

CHINESE

Conversational Chinese Dialogues: 50 Chinese Conversations and Short Stories

GERMAN

Conversational German Dialogues: 50 German Conversations and Short Stories

WANT THE NEXT ITALIAN BOOK FOR FREE?

https://touri.co/premium-access-italian-dialogues/

INTRODUCTION

So you're ready to take the plunge and learn Italian? What an excellent choice you have made to expand your horizons and open more doors of opportunities in your life.

If this is your first time or a continuation in your Italian learning journey, we want you to know that we're proud of you.

Italian is the fourth most widely spoken first language in the European Union with 69 million native speakers, an astounding 13% of the EU population and it is spoken as a second language by 16 million EU citizens. Including Italian speakers in non-EU European countries (such as Switzerland and Albania) and on other continents, the total number of speakers is around 90 million. Additionally, it is also the fourth most studied language in the world, which is impressive due to its relatively small country size.

As you may know, learning a new language has a multitude of benefits that expand far beyond simply navigating through a conversation with a native speaker. The ability to communicate in a foreign language will allow you to truly immerse yourself in different cultures, create even more memorable travel experiences and become even more marketable for advancements in career opportunities.

It is human nature to naturally progress and learn from the day we are born. Since birth we have been shaping our preferences based on our previous experiences. These experiences have provided you important feedback about your likes, dislikes, what has made you better or worse and allowed you to learn from these lessons.

The same approach should be taken to learn a new language.

Our goal with this book is to provide engaging and fun learning material that is relevant and useful in the real Italian-speaking world. Some students are provided with difficult or boring language materials that cause the learner to become overwhelmed and give up shortly after.

Building a strong foundation of vocabulary is critical to your improvement and reaching fluency. We *guarantee* you that this book is packed with vocabulary and phrases that you can start using today.

WHAT THIS BOOK IS ABOUT & HOW IT WORKS

A sure-fire way to exponentially decrease your time to Italian fluency is to role play with key words and phrases that naturally occur in actual scenarios you experience on a daily basis.

This book has 50 examples of conversations, written in both Italian and English so you never feel lost in translation, and will ensure you boost your conversational skills quickly.

You will find each chapter different from the last as two or more characters interact in real life scenarios. You will soon learn how to ask for directions, send a package at the post office, call for help, introduce yourself and even order at a restaurant.

Sometimes a direct translation does not make sense to and from each language. Therefore, we recommend that you read each story in both languages to ensure understanding what is taking place.

TIPS FOR SUCCESS

No doubt you can pick up this book at anytime to reference a situation that you may be in. However, in order to get the most out of this book, there is an effective approach to yield the best results.

1. **Role-play:** Learning takes place when activities are engaging and memorable. Role-play is any speaking activity when you either put yourself into someone else's shoes, or when put yourself into an imaginary situation and act it out.

2. **Look up vocab:** At some points there may be a word or phrase that you don't understand and that's completely fine. As we mentioned before, some of the translations are not word-for-word in order for the conversations to remain realistic in each language. Therefore, we recommend that you look up anything that is not fully clear to you.

3. **Create your own conversations:** After going through all of the stories we invite you to create your own by modifying what you already read. Perhaps you order additional items while at a restaurant or maybe you have an entirely different conversation over the phone. Let your imagination run wild.

4. **Seek out more dialogues:** Don't let your learning stop here. We encourage you to practice in as many ways as possible. Referencing your newly learned phrases and vocabulary, you can test your comprehension with Italian movies and television shows. Practice, practice, practice will give you the boost to fluency.

Focus on building your foundation of words and phrases commonly used in the real world and we promise your results will be staggering! Now, go out into the world, speak with confidence and in no time native speakers will be amazed by your Italian speaking skills.

Good luck!

BASIC SURVIVAL PHRASES

GREETINGS

1. *Salve!* – **Hello [any time of day]**
    (sal-vay)

2. *Salve, come va?* – **Hello, how are you?**
    (sal-vay ko-may va?)

3. *Buongiorno* – **Good morning**
    (bu-on-jour-no)

4. *Buon pomeriggio* – **Good afternoon**
    (bu-on po-mer-eej-jio)

5. *Buonasera* – **Good evening**
    (bu-on-a-say-ra)

6. *Buonanotte* – **Good night**
    (bu-ona-not-tay)

7. *Grazie mille* – **Thank you very much**
    (gra-tsee mee-lay)

8. *Grazie a Lei* – Thank you, too [replying to "thank you" from someone else]

   (gra-tsee a lay)

9. *Arrivederci, alla prossima* – Goodbye, see you next time

   (arr-ee-va-der-chee al-la pros-see-ma)

10. *Mi chiamo...* – My name is _

    (mee kee-amo)

11. *Sono americano/canadese/inglese* – I'm American/Canadian/English

    (so-no am-er-ee-kah-no / kan-a-day-say / een-glay-say)

12. *Lei di dov'è?* – Where are you from?

    (lay dee do-vay?)

13. *Piacere* – Nice to meet you

    (pee-a-chay-ray)

14. *Mi sto divertendo molto* – I'm having a great time!

    (mee sto dee-ver-ten-do mol-to)

15. *Parla inglese?* – Do you speak English?

    (par-la een-glay-say?)

16. *Mi scusi* – I'm sorry
    (mee skoo-see)

17. *Non lo so* – I don't know

    (non lo so)

18. *Va bene* – All right

(va be-nay)

19. *Non importa* – Never mind

(non eem-por-ta)

20. *Cosa vuole dire?* – What does that mean?

(ko-sa vu-ol-ay dee-ray?)

21. *Non parlo italiano molto bene* – I don't speak Italian very well

(non par-lo ital-ee-ah-no mol-to beh-nay)

22. *Mi scusi, non capisco* – I don't understand!

(mee scoo-see non ka-pee-sko)

23. *Potrebbe ripetere, per favore?* – Could you say that again please?

(po-tre-bay ree-peh-teh-reh per fa-vawr-ay)

24. *Potrebbe scrivermelo?* – Please write that down for me

(po-tre-bay skree-ver-may-lo?)

25. *Bella giornata oggi, vero?* – The weather is lovely today, isn't it?

(bella jee-or-na-ta ojji vay-ro?)

RESTAURANT

1. *Un tavolo per uno / due, per favore* – **A table for one / two please**

   (oon ta-vo-lo per oo=no / doo-ay, per fa-vo-ray?)

2. *Siete già aperti?* – **Are you open yet?**

   (see-et-ay jee-ah a-per-tee?)

3. *Possiamo aspettare (per un tavolo)?* – **Can we wait (for a table)?**

   (poss-ee-amo as-pett-ah-ray per oon ta-va-lo?)

4. *Cos'è questo?* – **What's this?**

   (ko-say kwes-to?)

5. *Possiamo sederci laggiù?* – **Can we sit over there?**

   (poss-ee-amo se-der-chee la-jee-oo)

6. *Mi scusi!* – **Excuse me! [Calling a waiter]**

   (mee skoo-see)

7. *Potrei avere il menu, per favore?* – **Can I have the menu, please?**

   pot-ray a-vay-ray eel me-noo, per fa-vo-ray?)

8. *Cosa mi consiglia?* – **What do you recommend?**

   (ko-sa mee kon-sihl-ya?)

9. *Qual è la specialità della casa?* – What's your most popular dish?

    (Kwal e la spe-chee-a-lee-tay de-la ka-sa?)

10. *Il conto, per favore* – The cheque, please

    (il kon-to, per fa-vor-ay)

TRANSPORTATION

1. *Vorrei andare a __ – I want to go to _*
   (vo-ray an-da-ray a _)

2. *A che ora parte il prossimo treno/autobus per __?* - What time is the next train/bus to _ ?
   (a kay oh-ra par-tay eel pros-see-mo tray-no / auw-to-boos per _?)

3. *Quanto costa? – How much is it?*
   (kwan-to kos-ta?)

4. *1 biglietto / 2 biglietti (per __, per favore – 1 ticket / 2 tickets (to ___), please*
   (oon bil-yeto / doo-ah bil-yetti per _, per fa-vo-ray)

5. *Quanto dura il viaggio? – How long does it take?*
   (kwan-to doo-ra eel vi-ahj-o)

6. *Dove devo andare adesso? – Where should I go now?*
   (do-vay day-vo an-da-ray a-day-sso?)

7. *Quando parte? – When does it leave?*
   (kwan-do par-tay?)

8. *Che ore sono (adesso)? – What time is it (now)?*
   (kay ora so-no a-day-sso?)

9. *Questo treno/autobus ferma a __? –* **Does this train/bus stop in _?**

   (kwes-to tray-no / auw-to-boos fer-ma a _?)

10. *Mi scusi, è qui __? –* **Excuse me, is this _? [Useful when you're on the bus/train and aren't sure when to get off]**

    (mee skoo-see, ee kwee _?)

11. *Dove si trova _____ sulla carta? –* **Where is _____ on the map?**

    (do-vay see tro-va _ soo-la kar-ta?)

NUMBERS

1. **uno** – one
   (oo-no)
2. **due** – two
   (doo-ay)
3. **tre** – three
   (tray)
4. **quattro** – four
   (kwat-ro)
5. **cinque** – five
   (chee-kway)
6. **sei** – six
   (say)
7. **sette** – seven
   (say-tay)
8. **otto** – eight
   (ot-to)
9. **nove** – nine
   (no-vay)
10. **dieci** – ten
    (dee-ay-chee)
11. **undici** – eleven
    (oon-dee-chee)
12. **dodici** – twelve
    (do-dee-chee)

13. tredici – thirteen

(tray-dee-chee)

14. quattordici – fourteen

(kwa-tor-dee-chee)

15. quindici – fifteen

(kween-dee-chee)

16. sedici – sixteen

(say-dee-chee)

17. diciassette – seventeen

(dee-chee-a-set-tay)

18. diciotto – eighteen

(dee-chee-ot-to)

19. diciannove – nineteen

(dee-chee-no-vay)

20. venti – twenty

(ven-tee)

21. ventuno – twenty-one

(ven-too-no)

22. ventidue – twenty-two

(ven-tee-doo-ay)

23. trenta – thirty

(tren-ta)

24. quaranta – forty

(kwa-ran-ta)

25. cinquanta – fifty

(cheen-kwan-ta)

26. sessanta – sixty

(ses-san-ta)

27. settanta – seventy

(se-ten-ta)

28. ottanta – eighty

(o-tan-ta)

29. novanta – ninety

(no-van-ta)

30. cento – one hundred

(chen-to)

31. duecentocinquanta – two hundred and fifty

(doo-ay-chen-to-cheen-kwan-ta)

32. cinquecento – five hundred

(cheen-kway-chen-to)

33. mille – one thousand

(mee-lay)

1. Saluto Formale – Formal Greeting

Giovanni: Buongiorno, Professor Paolo, come sta?

Professor Paolo: Buongiorno, Giovanni. Sto bene. E lei?

Giovanni: Tutto bene, grazie. Questa è la mia amica Clarissa. Sta pensando di iscriversi a questa università. Ha delle domande da porle. È così gentile da poterle spiegare come fare?

Professor Paolo: Ciao, Clarissa! È un piacere conoscerla. Sono felice di poterla aiutare. Per cortesia, venga a trovarmi nel mio ufficio la prossima settimana.

Clarissa: È un piacere conoscerla, professore. Grazie mille per avermi aiutato.

Professor Paolo: Si figuri. Spero di poter rispondere a tutte le sue domande!

FORMAL GREETING

Giovanni: Good morning, Professor Justin, how are you doing?

Professor Paolo: Good morning, Giovanni. I am doing well. And you?

Giovanni: I'm well, thank you. This is my friend Clarissa. She is thinking about applying to this university. She has a few questions. Would you mind telling us about the process, please?

Professor Paolo: Hello, Clarissa! It's a pleasure to meet you. I'm more than happy to speak with you. Please stop by my office next week.

Clarissa: It's a pleasure to meet you, professor. Thank you so much for helping us.

Professor Paolo: Of course. Hopefully, I will be able to answer your questions!

2. Saluto Informale – Informal Greeting

Nicola: Chi è la donna alta accanto a Barbara?

Carlo: è la sua amica Maria. Non l'hai incontrata alla festa di Steve?

Nicola: No, non sono andato alla festa di Steve.

Carlo: Oh! Allora aspetta che ti presento ora. Maria, questo è il mio amico Nicola.

Maria: Ciao, Nicola. Piacere di conoscerti.

Nicola: Anche per me. Vuoi bere qualcosa?

Maria: Certo, andiamo.

INFORMAL GREETING

Nicola: Who's the tall woman next to Barbara?

Carlo: That's her friend Mary. Didn't you meet her at Steve's party?

Nicola: No, I wasn't at Steve's party.

Carlo: Oh! Then let me introduce you to her now. Mary, this is my friend Nicola.

Maria: Hi, Nicola. Nice to meet you.

Nicola: You, too. Would you like a drink?

Maria: Sure, let's go get one.

3. Una Chiamata Telefonica – A Telephone Call

Giovanni: Ciao Alice, sono Giovanni. Come stai?

Alice: Oh, ciao, Giovanni! Ti stavo pensando.

Giovanni: Che carina. Mi stavo chiedendo se ti piacerebbe andare a vedere un film stasera.

Alice: Certo, mi piacerebbe! Quale film vorresti vedere?

Giovanni: Pensavo di andare a vedere la nuova commedia:" Spegni le luci". Cosa ne pensi?

Alice: Sembra interessante!

Giovanni: Ok, ti vengo a prendere alle 7:30. Il film inizia alle 8:00.

Alice: a dopo. Ciao!

A TELEPHONE CALL

Giovanni: Hi, Alice, it's Giovanni. How are you?

Alice: Oh, hi, Giovanni! I was just thinking about you.

Giovanni: That's nice. I was wondering if you'd like to go to a movie tonight.

Alice: Sure, I'd love to! Which movie do you want to see?

Giovanni: I was thinking about that new comedy *Turn Off the Lights*. What do you think?

Alice: Sounds great!

Giovanni: Ok, I'll pick you up around 7:30. The movie starts at 8:00.

Alice: See you then. Bye!

4. CHE ORE SONO? – WHAT TIME IS IT?

Federica: che ore sono? Siamo in ritardo!

Antonio: Sono le sette e un quarto. Siamo in orario. Non essere ansiosa.

Federica: pensavo che dovessimo stare al ristorante alle 7:30, per la festa a sorpresa. Non ce la faremo mai con tutto il traffico che c'è stasera.

Antonio: Sono sicuro che ce la faremo. L'ora di punta è quasi finita. Comunque, la festa inizia alle 8:00.

Ma avrei bisogno delle giuste indicazioni. Puoi chiamare il ristorante e chiedere dove possiamo parcheggiare la macchina?

Federica: certo.

WHAT TIME IS IT?

Federica: What time is it? We're going to be late!

Antonio: It's a quarter after seven. We're on time. Don't panic.

Federica: But I thought we had to be at the restaurant by 7:30 for the surprise party. We'll never make it there with all this evening traffic.

Antonio: I'm sure we will. Rush hour is almost over. Anyway, the party starts at 8:00.

But I do need help with directions. Can you call the restaurant and ask them where we park our car?

Federica: Of course.

5. PUOI RIPETERE? – CAN YOU SAY THAT AGAIN?

Luca: Ciao! Ciao, Stefania, come vanno le cose in ufficio?

Stefania: Ciao, Luca! Come stai? Per favore, puoi fermarti al negozio e comprare una risma di carta per la stampante?

Luca: cosa hai detto? Puoi ripetere per favore? Hai detto di prendere le cartucce per la stampante? Scusami, ma il telefono non prende bene.

Stefania: Ora mi senti? No, ho bisogno di più carta per il computer. Ascolta, ti scrivo esattamente quello che mi serve. Grazie, Luca. Ci sentiamo più tardi.

Luca: Grazie, Stefania. Scusami, ma qui il telefono ha una pessima ricezione.

CAN YOU SAY THAT AGAIN?

Luca: Hello? Hi, Stefania, how are things at the office?

Stefania: Hi, Luca! How are you? Can you please stop at the store and pick up extra paper for the printer?

Luca: What did you say? Can you repeat that, please? Did you say to pick up ink for the printer? Sorry, the phone is cutting out.

Stefania: Can you hear me now? No, I need more computer paper. Listen, I'll text you exactly what I need. Thanks, Luca.

Talk to you later.

Luca: Thanks, Stefania. Sorry, my phone has really bad

reception here.

6. Coincidenze – Coincidences

Martina: ehi Giulia, ciao! Da quanto tempo!

Giulia: Martina! Ciao! Che coincidenza! Non ti vedo da un secolo! Cosa ci fai qui?

Martina: Ho da poco ottenuto un nuovo lavoro in città e ne sto approfittando per comprare qualche vestito. Ehi, cosa ne pensi di questa maglietta?

Giulia: Hmmm ... Beh, sai bene quanto mi piace il blu. Guarda? Ho la maglietta dello stesso colore!

Martina: Hai sempre avuto buon gusto! Come è piccolo il mondo.

COINCIDENCES

Martina: Well, hello there, Giulia! Long time no see!

Giulia: Martina! Hi! What a coincidence! I haven't seen you in forever! What are you doing here?

Martina: I just got a new job in the city, so I'm shopping for some clothes. Hey, what do you think of this shirt?

Giulia: Hmmm... Well, you know how much I love blue. See? I've got the same shirt!

Martina: You always did have good taste! What a small world.

7. Il Meteo – The Weather

Emma: Si gela fuori! Cosa gli è preso al tempo? Pensavo che questo freddo sarebbe finito.

Gabriella: Sì, lo pensavo anch'io. È quello che stamattina ho letto online.

Emma: Penso che il vento freddo stia decisamente abbassando la temperatura.

Gabriella: Possiamo andare dentro? Non sento più i miei piedi.

THE WEATHER

Emma: It's freezing outside! What happened to the weather report? I thought this cold front was supposed to pass.

Gabriella: Yeah, I thought so too. That's what I read online this morning.

Emma: I guess the wind chill is really driving down the temperature.

Gabriella: Can we go inside? I feel like my toes are starting to go numb.

8. ORDINANDO DEL CIBO – ORDERING FOOD

Cameriere: Ciao, oggi sarò il vostro cameriere. Posso iniziare a portarvi qualcosa da bere?

Fabio: Sì. Vorrei del tè freddo, per favore.

Anna: per me limonata, per favore.

Cameriere: Ok. Siete già pronti ad ordinare o avete bisogno di qualche altro minuto?

Fabio: siamo pronti. Per iniziare prendo la zuppa di pomodoro e il roast beef con purè di patate e piselli.

Cameriere: come gradisce la cottura del manzo: al sangue, media o ben cotta?

Fabio: Ben cotta, per favore.

Anna: Per me pesce, con patate ed insalata.

ORDERING FOOD

Waiter: Hello, I'll be your waiter today. Can I start you off with something to drink?

Fabio: Yes. I would like iced tea, please.

Anna: And I'll have lemonade., please.

Waiter: Ok. Are you ready to order, or do you need a few minutes?

Fabio: I think we're ready. I'll have the tomato soup to start, and the roast beef with mashed potatoes and peas.

Waiter: How do you want the beef — rare, medium, or well done?

Fabio: Well done, please.

Anna: And I'll just have the fish, with potatoes and a salad.

9. VISITA DAL DOTTORE – VISITING THE DOCTOR

Dottore: Qual è il suo problema?

Catia: Beh ... ho una brutta tosse e mal di gola. Inoltre ho mal di testa.

Dottore: Da quanto tempo ha questi sintomi?

Catia: da circa tre giorni e mi sento anche molto stanco.

Dottore: Hmm. Sembra che lei abbia preso l'influenza. Prenda una compressa di aspirina ogni quattro ore e si riposi. Si assicuri di bere molto. Mi chiami la prossima settimana se dovesse essere ancora malato.

Catia: D'accordo, la ringrazio.

VISITING THE DOCTOR

Doctor: What seems to be the problem?

Catia: Well... I have a bad cough and a sore throat. I also have a headache.

Doctor: How long have you had these symptoms?

Catia: About three days now. And I'm really tired, too.

Doctor: Hmm. It sounds like you've got the flu. Take aspirin every four hours and get plenty of rest. Make sure you drink lots of fluids. Call me if you're still sick next week.

Catia: Ok, thank you.

10. Chiedere Indicazioni – Asking For Directions

Marco: Mi scusi. Potrebbe dirmi dov'è la biblioteca?

Olivia: Certo. Prosegua per tre isolati a Washington Street e poi giri a destra. È all'angolo, di fronte alla banca.

Marco: Grazie mille! Sono in città da pochi giorni e non so ancora come muovermi.

Olivia: Oh, so bene come si sente. Ci siamo trasferiti qui un anno fa, e ancora non la conosco tutta!

ASKING FOR DIRECTIONS

Marco: Excuse me. Could you tell me where the library is?

Olivia: Yes, it's that way. You go three blocks to Washington Street, then turn right. It's on the corner, across from the bank.

Marco: Thanks! I've only been in town a few days, so I really don't know my way around yet.

Olivia: Oh, I know how you feel. We moved here a year ago, and I still don't know where everything is!

11. Chiamata Di Emergenza – Calling For Help

Piero: ehi! Da quell'auto è uscita una fiammata e poco dopo si è scontrata con quel camion!

Alessandra: Qualcuno è rimasto ferito?

Piero: Non lo so ... chiamiamo il 118... Pronto? Vorrei segnalare un incidente stradale vicino all'ufficio postale in via Houston. Sembra ci sia un uomo ferito. Sì, è appena successo. Ok grazie. Ciao.

Alessandra: cosa hanno detto?

Piero: manderanno subito un'ambulanza e una pattuglia dei carabinieri.

Alessandra: ottimo, sono arrivati. Spero che quell'uomo stia bene.

Piero: Speriamo. Devi stare molto attento quando guidi.

CALLING FOR HELP

Piero: Hey! That car just ran a red light and hit that truck!

Alessandra: Is anyone hurt?

Piero: I don't know... let's call 911. ...Hello? I'd like to report a car accident near the post office on Houston Street. It looks like a man is hurt. Yes, it just happened. Ok, thanks. Bye.

Alessandra: What did they say?

Piero: They're going to send an ambulance and a police car right away.

Alessandra: Good, they're here. I hope the man is alright.

Piero: I know. You have to be so careful when you're driving.

12. Acquisti – Shopping

Luisa: ehi, Giulia ... guarda quei dessert! Che ne dici di preparare dei biscotti oggi?

Giulia: Hmm ... Sì, è una grande idea! Visto che siamo qui, prendiamo gli ingredienti.

Giulia: Ok, cosa ci serve?

Luisa: farina, zucchero e burro. Oh, e abbiamo anche bisogno delle uova e delle gocce di cioccolato.

Giulia: Perché non prendi gli ingredienti caseari? Li trovi negli scomparti refrigerati nel retro del negozio. Io prenderò gli altri ingredienti. Credo che siano nel corridoio 10.

Luisa: ottimo! Incontriamoci alla cassa.

Giulia: Ok. Ci vediamo lì.

SHOPPING

Luisa: Hey, Giulia... Look at those desserts! How about baking some cookies today?

Giulia: Hmm... Yeah, that's a great idea! While we're here, let's pick up the ingredients.

Giulia: Ok, what do we need?

Luisa: The recipe calls for flour, sugar and butter. Oh, and we also need eggs and chocolate chips.

Giulia: Why don't you get the dairy ingredients? You'll find those in the refrigerated section in the back of the store. I'll get the dry ingredients. I believe they're in aisle 10.

Luisa: Great! Let's meet at the checkout.

Giulia: Ok. See you there.

13. COMMISSIONI – RUNNING ERRANDS

Addetto alla reception dell'hotel: Ciao. Come posso aiutarla?

Chiara: Resterò qui in città per qualche giorno e nel frattempo dovrò fare alcune cose.

Addetto alla reception dell'hotel: certamente. Di che cosa ha bisogno?

Chiara: Dovrei tagliarmi i capelli. Ho anche bisogno di un'orlatura per i miei nuovi pantaloni.

Personale dell'albergo: d'accordo. Ecco una mappa della città. C'è un buon parrucchiere in zona, a solo un isolato da qui. E abbiamo un sarto qui. C'è niente altro che posso fare per lei?

Chiara: Sì. Prima del lungo viaggio di ritorno ho bisogno di far riparare la mia auto!

Addetto alla reception dell'hotel: nessun problema. C'è un buon meccanico a pochi isolati da qui.

RUNNING ERRANDS

Hotel receptionist: Hello there. How can I help you?

Chiara: Well, I'm in town visiting for a few days, and I need to get some things done while I'm here.

Hotel receptionist: Sure. What do you need?

Chiara: I need to get my hair cut. I also need to have my new pants hemmed.

Hotel receptionist: Ok. Here's a map of the city. There's a good hair salon here, which is just a block away. And there's a tailor right here. Is there anything else?

Chiara: Yes. I'll need to get my car serviced before my long drive back home!

Hotel receptionist: No problem. There's a good mechanic a few blocks away.

14. All'ufficio Postale – At The Post Office

Impiegato postale: come posso aiutarla?

Carola: Gentilmente, ho bisogno di spedire questo pacco a New York.

Impiegato postale: Ok, vediamo quanto pesa ... è di circa cinque libbre. Se lo invia con il corriere espresso, arriverà domani. Oppure può inviarla con la posta prioritaria e arriverà entro sabato.

Carola: sabato va più che bene. Qual è il costo?

Impiegato postale: 12,41 sterline. Ha bisogno di altro?

Carola: Oh, sì! Quasi dimenticavo. Mi serve anche un libro per i francobolli.

Impiegato postale: Ok, il totale ammonta a 18,94 sterline.

AT THE POST OFFICE

Postal clerk: What can I help you today?

Carola: I need to mail this package to New York, please.

Postal clerk: Ok, let's see how much it weighs... it's about five pounds. If you send it express, it will get there tomorrow. Or you can send it priority and it will get there by Saturday.

Carola: Saturday is fine. How much will that be?

Postal clerk: $12.41. Do you need anything else?

Carola: Oh, yeah! I almost forgot. I need a book of stamps, too.

Postal clerk: Ok, your total comes to $18.94.

15. L'esame – The Exam

Bianca: ehi! Come è andato l'esame di fisica?

Franco: benone, grazie. Sono solo contento che sia finita! E a te invece ... come è andata la presentazione?

Bianca: Oh, è andata davvero bene. Grazie per avermi aiutato!

Franco: Nessun problema. Hai voglia domani di studiare insieme per l'esame di matematica?

Bianca: Sì, volentieri! Vieni verso le 10:00, dopo la colazione.

Franco: Va bene. Porterò i miei appunti.

THE EXAM

Bianca: Hey! How did your physics exam go?

Franco: Not bad, thanks. I'm just glad it's over! How about your... how'd your presentation go?

Bianca: Oh, it went really well. Thanks for helping me with it!

Franco: No problem. So... do you feel like studying tomorrow for our math exam?

Bianca: Yeah, sure! Come over around 10:00 am, after breakfast.

Franco: All right. I'll bring my notes.

16. Il Maglione Perfetto – The Perfect Sweater

Negoziante: Posso aiutarla?

Gloria: Sì, sto cercando un maglione – taglia M.

Negoziante: Vediamo ... eccone uno di color bianco. Cosa ne pensi?

Gloria: se è possibile vorrei vederlo blu.

Negoziante: Ok ... ecco quello blu, taglia M. Vorresti provarlo?

Gloria: certo ... sì, lo adoro. Mi sta alla perfezione. Quanto costa?

Negoziante: costa 41 sterline, con le tasse arriviamo a 50.

Gloria: perfetto! Lo prendo. La ringrazio!

THE PERFECT SWEATER

Salesperson: Can I help you?

Gloria: Yes, I'm looking for a sweater — in a size medium.

Salesperson: Let's see... here's a nice white one. What do you think?

Gloria: I think I'd rather have it in blue.

Salesperson: Ok ... here's blue, in a medium. Would you like to try it on?

Gloria: Ok ... yes, I love it. It fits perfectly. How much is it?

Salesperson: It's $41. It will be $50, with tax.

Gloria: Perfect! I'll take it. Thank you!

17. Taxi o Bus – Taxi Or Bus

Lara: prendiamo un taxi o un autobus per andare al cinema?

Lorenzo: Prendiamo l'autobus. È impossibile prendere un taxi durante l'ora di punta.

Lara: ma quella non è una fermata dell'autobus?

Lorenzo: Sì ... Oh! C'è un autobus. Dobbiamo correre per prenderlo.

Lara: Oh, no! L'abbiamo perso.

Lorenzo: Nessun problema. Ce ne sarà un altro tra 10 minuti.

TAXI OR BUS

Lara: Should we take a taxi or a bus to the movie theater?

Lorenzo: Let's take a bus. It's impossible to get a taxi during rush hour.

Lara: Isn't that a bus stop over there?

Lorenzo: Yes... Oh! There's a bus now. We'll have to run to catch it.

Lara: Oh, no! We just missed it.

Lorenzo: No problem. There'll be another one in 10 minutes.

18. QUANTI ANNI HAI – HOW OLD ARE YOU?

Gloria: Sono davvero eccitata per la festa a sorpresa per il compleanno della zia di Barbara, questo pomeriggio! E tu?

Nadia: Sì! Quanti anni fa?

Gloria: farà 55 anni il 5 maggio.

Nadia: Wow! Non pensavo che mia madre fosse più grande – ne farà 58 il 9 ottobre. In ogni caso, zia Maria sarà molto sorpresa di vederci!

Gloria: lo so! Ma dobbiamo ancora preparare tutto prima che arrivi ... Ok! Siamo tutti pronti. Shh! è qui!

Tutti: sorpresa!

HOW OLD ARE YOU?

Gloria: I'm really excited for Aunt Mary's surprise birthday party this afternoon! Aren't you?

Nadia: Yeah! How old is she?

Gloria: She'll be 55 on May 5.

Nadia: Wow! I didn't know that my mom was older — she's going to be 58 on October 9. Anyway, Aunt Mary's going to be so surprised to see us all here!

Gloria: I know! But we still have to get all the food set up before she gets here ... Ok! We're all ready now. Shh! She's here!

All: Surprise!

19. AL TEATRO – AT THE THEATER

Vincenzo: per favore, mi dia due biglietti per lo spettacolo delle 3:30.

Vendita biglietti: Ecco a lei, Buona visione!

[All'interno del teatro]

Vincenzo: Ti dispiacerebbe scalare, così io e il mio amico possiamo sederci vicini?

Donna: No, figurati.

Vincenzo: Grazie mille!

At The Theater

Vincenzo: We'd like two tickets for the 3:30 show, please.

Ticket sales: Here you go. Enjoy the movie!

[Inside the theater]

Vincenzo: Would you mind moving over one, so my friend and I can sit together?

Woman: No, not at all.

Vincenzo: Thank you so much!

20. Cosa Sai Fare?– What Are You Good At Doing?

Sandra: Allora ... cosa facciamo?

Pamela: Beh, mi piace l'arte e sono davvero bravo nel disegno. Che ne pensi?

Sandra: Hmm ... che ne dici di giocare a un gioco da tavolo? Sarebbe più divertente.

Pamela: Ok. Giochiamo a Scrabble! Sono davvero bravo anche nello spelling!

Sandra: Oh, davvero? Lo vedremo!

WHAT ARE YOU GOOD AT DOING?

Sandra: So ... what should we do?

Pamela: Well, I like to do arts and crafts, and I'm really good at drawing. What do you think?

Sandra: Hmm ... how about playing a board game? That would be more fun.

Pamela: Ok. Let's play Scrabble! I'm really good at spelling, too!

Sandra: Oh, yeah? We'll see about that!

21. Qual'è Il Tuo Sport Preferito – What Is Your Favorite Sport?

Filippo: A che ora inizia la partita di calcio? Pensavo fosse già iniziata a mezzogiorno.

Pasquale: abbiamo sbagliato l'orario. Oh, comunque il calcio non è lo sport che prediligo. Preferisco di gran lunga il basket.

Filippo: Oh, davvero? Pensavo che il tuo sport preferito fosse il tennis! Anche a me piace molto il basket.

Pasquale: che ne pensi di giocarci prima o poi?

Filippo: certo! Perché non facciamo adesso qualche tiro libero dato che la partita di calcio non è ancora iniziata?

Pasquale: ottima idea. Andiamo.

What Is Your Favorite Sport?

Filippo: What time is that soccer game on? I thought it started at noon.

Pasquale: We must have had the wrong time. Oh, well ... soccer's not my favorite sport anyway. I much prefer basketball.

Filippo: Oh, really? I thought your favorite sport was tennis! I'm a big fan of basketball, too.

Pasquale: How about a game sometime?

Filippo: Sure thing! Why don't we go shoot some hoops now since the soccer game isn't on?

Pasquale: Excellent idea. Let's go.

22. ANDARE A VEDERE UN MUSICAL – GOING TO SEE A MUSICAL

Leandra: Che spettacolo fantastico! Grazie per avermi invitato al musical.

Elena: Sono contento che ti sia piaciuto. La coreografia dei ballerini è stata incredibile. Mi ha fatto ricordare quando tanti anni fa ballavo.

Leandra: immagino! Eri una ballerina così talentuosa. Ti manca molto ballare?

Elena: Oh, sei gentile, Leandra. A volte mi manca ma avrò sempre l'interesse per l'arte. Ecco perché amo andare ai musical perché è la combinazione perfetta di danza, musica e teatro.

Leandra: assolutamente! Sono contenta che tu sia ancora appassionata d'arte. Grazie per l'invito. È sempre un piacere assistere ad un evento artistico con te e imparare qualcosa di nuovo.

GOING TO SEE A MUSICAL

Leandra: What a fantastic performance! Thank you for inviting me to the musical.

Elena: You are welcome. I'm happy you enjoyed the show. The choreography of the dancers was incredible. It reminds me of when I used to dance many years ago.

Leandra: I know! You were such a talented ballerina. Do you miss dancing?

Elena: Oh, that's very kind of you, Leandra. I do miss it sometimes. But I will always be a fan of the arts. That's why I love going to musicals because it's the perfect combination of dance, song and theater.

Leandra: Absolutely! I'm glad you are still an art fan too. Thank you for the invitation. It's always a pleasure to attend an arts event with you and learn something new.

23. Fare Una Vacanza – Taking A Vacation

Gemma: ho appena comprato un biglietto per New York. Sono così entusiasta di vedere la città!

Sofia: Buon per te! Viaggiare è così bello. Adoro scoprire nuovi posti e nuove persone. Quando parti?

Gemma: la prossima settimana. Sto prendendo il volo di notte. Era quello più economico. Spero di riuscire a dormire sull'aereo.

Sofia: vorrei poter venire con te! New York City è un posto magico. Ti divertirai tanto.

Gemma: lo spero. Vado a trovare mio fratello che vive lì. Starò una settimana e poi prenderò il treno fino a Washington, DC

Sofia: Sembra una bella vacanza. Io invece non vedo l'ora di passare una settimana in spiaggia per le mie vacanze estive. Voglio solo rilassarmi.

TAKING A VACATION

Gemma: I just bought a ticket to New York City. I'm so excited to see the city!

Sofia: Good for you! Traveling is so much fun. I love discovering new places and new people. When are you leaving?

Gemma: Next week. I'm taking the red eye. It was cheaper. Hopefully, I'll be able to sleep on the plane.

Sofia: I wish I could go with you! New York City is a magical place. You will have so much fun.

Gemma: I hope so. I'm going to visit my brother who lives there. I will stay for a week and then take the train down to Washington, DC

Sofia: That sounds like a great vacation. I'm looking forward to a week at the beach for my summer vacation. I just want to relax.

24. AL NEGOZIO DI ANIMALI – AT THE PET STORE

Alessia: che bel gatto! Cosa ne dici?

Gabriele: preferirei prendere un cane. I cani sono più fedeli dei gatti, che sono solo pigri.

Alessia: Sì, ma hanno bisogno di tanta attenzione! Saresti disposto a portarlo a spasso tutti i giorni? E pulirlo?

Gabriele: Hmm. Ottima domanda. Che ne dici di un uccello? O di un pesciolino?

Alessia: Dovremmo spendere un bel po' di soldi per la gabbia o per acquistare un acquario. E onestamente non so come ci si prende cura di un uccello o di un pesce!

Gabriele: Beh, chiaramente non siamo ancora pronti per avere un animale domestico.

Alessia: Haha ... Sì, hai ragione. Prendiamo qualcosa da mangiare e ne riparliamo.

AT THE PET STORE

Alessia: What a beautiful cat! What do you think?

Gabriele: I think I'd rather get a dog. Dogs are more loyal than cats. Cats are just lazy.

Alessia: Yes, but they need so much attention! Would you be willing to walk it every single day? And clean up after it?

Gabriele: Hmm. Good point. What about a bird? Or a fish?

Alessia: We'd have to invest a lot of money in a cage or a fish tank. And I honestly don't know how to take care of a bird or a fish!

Gabriele: Well, we're obviously not ready to get a pet yet.

Alessia: Haha... Yeah, you're right. Let's get some food and talk about it.

25. Esprimendo La Tua Opinione – Expressing Your Opinion

Orazio: Dove andiamo in vacanza quest'anno? Dobbiamo decidere in fretta.

Maria: Beh, mi piacerebbe andare in un posto dove fa caldo. Che ne dici della spiaggia? O potremmo affittare una casina sul lago.

Orazio: di nuovo in spiaggia? Quest'inverno vorrei andare a sciare. Possiamo venirci in contro e il prossimo Aprile andare in Colorado sulle Montagne Rocciose? Li ci sono delle bellissime località sciistiche.

Maria: Oh, non siamo mai stati in Colorado prima d'ora! Ma non so se fino ad allora farà ancora caldo. Devo prima fare qualche ricerca. Questo mi aiuterà a prendere una decisione.

EXPRESSING YOUR OPINION

Orazio: Where should we take a vacation this year? We need to decide soon.

Maria: Well, I'd like to go somewhere warm. How about the beach? Or we could rent a cabin on the lake.

Orazio: You want to go to the beach, again? I want to ski this winter. We can compromise and travel to the Rocky Mountains in Colorado next April? There are beautiful ski resorts there.

Maria: Oh, we've never been to Colorado before! But I don't know if it will be sunny and warm then. I need to do some research first. That will help me make a decision.

26. PASSATEMPI – HOBBIES

Rino: Sono così felice che questa settimana sia finita la sessione d'esami.

Michele: anch'io. Non vedo l'ora di rilassarmi in montagna questo fine settimana. Ho pianificato una bella escursione tra i boschi. Inoltre, se il tempo lo consente, ho intenzione di andare in canoa sul fiume.

Rino: Oh, che divertimento! Io vado nel Colorado. Ci andrò con la mia macchina fotografica perché si sta avvicinando l'autunno. In questo periodo le foglie cambiano il loro colore, prendendo sfumature rosse e arancione. Sarà bellissimo.

Michele: La prossima volta che andrai lì, ti raggiungerò. Ho sentito che il Colorado è un ottimo posto dove andare in canoa.

HOBBIES

Rino: I'm so happy this week of midterm exams is finished.

Michele: Same here. I'm looking forward to relaxing in the mountains this weekend. I've planned a nice little hike in the woods. Also, if the weather is good, I'm going to go canoeing down the river.

Rino: Oh, how fun! I'm going to Colorado. I'm taking my camera because fall is coming fast. The leaves are already turning all shades of red and orange. It will be awesome.

Michele: Next time you go there, I'll join you. I've heard Colorado is a great place to go canoeing.

27. Il Matrimonio – The Wedding

Angela: che bella la sposa con quell'abito, vero?

Maria: Sì. È incantevole. E lo sposo è così romantico.

Ho appena sentito la storia di come si sono fidanzati! Si dichiarò ad una cena a lume di candela, a Praga proprio dove andavano a scuola.

Angela: Davvero? Meraviglioso. E la luna di miele! Che bella idea hanno avuto! La maggior parte delle persone va soltanto in spiaggia una settimana dopo il fatidico si. Penso che sia un'idea così noiosa. Invece, hanno intenzione di andare in California e girare tutta la costa con la loro moto.

Maria: Davvero! Che idea fantastica. Questo è di gran lunga il miglior matrimonio che abbia mai visto in vita mia!

THE WEDDING

Angela: Doesn't the bride look beautiful in that wedding dress?

Maria: Yes. She looks amazing. And the groom is such a romantic.

I just heard the story of how they got engaged! He proposed to her during a candlelight dinner in Prague. That was where they went to school.

Angela: Oh yea? Wonderful. And the honeymoon! What a great idea! Most people just go to the beach for a week after they tie the knot. I think that's such a boring idea. Instead, they plan on going to California and cruising the coast on their motorcycle.

Maria: Really! What a fantastic idea. This is by far the best wedding I've ever been to in my life!

28. DARE CONSIGLI – GIVING ADVICE

Layla: Grazie di aver deciso di vedermi durante l'ora di pranzo. Lo apprezzo molto.

Monica: Nessun problema. Sono felice di aiutarti. Cosa succede?

Layla: Lo sai, le solite cose. Devo decidere in fretta ... Devo accettare questo nuovo lavoro oppure pensi che debba continuare con quello attuale?

Monica: Beh, penso che sia tempo di cambiare, giusto? Ti pagano con ritardo e sei infelice. Sono tutte ragioni valide per lasciare il tuo lavoro.

Layla: Lo pensi davvero?

Monica: si. ti ho ascoltato lamentarti per oltre un anno. Fidati di me. Accetta il lavoro. Cosa hai da perdere?

Layla: Ok, mi hai convinto. Mi hai sempre dato ottimi consigli.

GIVING ADVICE

Layla: Thanks for meeting with me during your lunch hour. I appreciate it.

Monica: No problem. I'm happy to help. What's happening?

Layla: Oh you know, the usual. I have to decide soon... Should I take this new job? Or do I stick with my current one?

Monica: Well, I think it's time for a change, don't you? They pay you late and you are unhappy. That's more than enough reasons to quit your job.

Layla: Do you really think so?

Monica: I know so. And I've been listening to you complain for over a year now. Trust me. Take the job. What do you have to lose?

Layla: Ok, you convinced me. You have always given me the best advice.

29. INSEGNARE AI BAMBINI – TEACHING CHILDREN

Samuele: Ciao Jack, come è andata la giornata?

Pasquale: Ciao Samuele, dove sei stato? Ti stavo cercando.

Samuele: Non crederai mai all'esperienza interessante che ho fatto. Sono stato tutto il giorno assieme ad un sacco di bambini!

Pasquale: Interessante. Dai racconta.

Samuele: Sì, è stato bello... ma anche molto estenuante! Non pensavo che i bambini avessero così tanta energia.

Pasquale: Dove hai incontrato tutti questi bambini?

Samuele: Alla scuola elementare di Chicago. In mattinata ho avuto l'opportunità di visitare alcune delle loro classi. Dopo di che, nel pomeriggio, gli ho insegnato un po' di inglese base usando dei giochi di parole.

Pasquale: Sono sicuro che l'inglese è stato probabilmente molto difficile per loro.

Samuele: Stranamente, erano tutti molto impazienti nel volerlo imparare. Onestamente, sono rimasto colpito.

Pasquale: ma è fantastico. Come ci sei riuscito?

Samuele: I bambini amano ripetere le cose ad alta voce! Così alcune volte gli dicevo le frasi con voce alta e loro le ripetevano gridando, altre volte invece le ho sussurrate e loro facevano altrettanto. È stato davvero divertente!

Pasquale: Sai, quando ero uno studente straniero, non abbiamo mai fatto delle lezioni di inglese in questo modo. Sono felice che i bambini abbiano fatto un'esperienza così bella.

TEACHING CHILDREN

Samuele: Hi Pasquale, how was your day?

Pasquale: Hi Samuele, where have you been? I've been looking for you.

Samuele: You won't believe the interesting experience I just had. I spent the whole day with a ton of children!

Pasquale: That sounds like fun. Tell me more.

Samuele: Yes, it was a great time... but it was so exhausting! I didn't realize that kids have so much energy.

Pasquale: Where did you meet all these kids?

Samuele: At the elementary school in Chicago. I had an opportunity to visit some of their classes in the morning. After that I taught them some basic English with word games in the afternoon.

Pasquale: I'm sure English was probably very difficult for them.

Samuele: Surprisingly, they were all very eager to learn. Honestly, I was impressed.

Pasquale: That's great. What did you end up teaching them?

Samuele: The kids love to repeat things out loud! Sometimes I yelled out the sentences, and they yelled back at me. I whispered, and they whispered back. It was so much fun!

Pasquale: You know, when I was a foreign exchange student, we never had English lessons like that. It makes me happy the children had such a wonderful experience.

30. Divertirsi Giocando A Tennis – Fun With Tennis

Alma: Sebastian, potresti mostrarmi come si tiene la racchetta?

Sebastian: Certo Alma, è proprio come quando ci stringiamo la mano. Tendi la mano come se stessi per stringermela...

Alma: Così?

Sebastian: Sì, proprio così. Ora prendi la racchetta in questo modo.

Alma: Ora sono pronta per colpire la palla come una professionista!

Sebastian: Haha, quasi! Ricorda cosa ti ho detto. Ci sono solo due tipi di swing, il dritto e il rovescio.

Alma: Ok, me lo ricorderò. Hai detto che per colpire di dritto, devo iniziare dalla mia destra ed è come colpire una pallina da ping pong.

Sebastian: vero. Provaci adesso. Sei pronti? Colpiscila!

Alma: Oops! L'ho completamente mancata!

Sebastian: non preoccuparti, riprova.

Alma: Ok, fammi riprovare...

Sebastian: arriva un'altra palla... Wow! È andata oltre il recinto! Sei una donna molto forte.

Alma: Haha. Dovrei allenarmi di più!

FUN WITH TENNIS

Alma: Sebastian, could you show me how to hold the racket?

Sebastian: Sure Alma, it's just like when we shake hands. Hold your hand out as if you were about to shake my hand...

Alma: Just like this?

Sebastian: Yes, just like that. Now, put the racket in your hand, like this.

Alma: Now I'm ready to hit the ball like a professional!

Sebastian: Haha, almost! Remember what I told you. There are only two types of swings, the forehand and the backhand.

Alma: Ok, I remember. You said hitting a forehand, starting on my right, is like hitting a ping pong ball.

Sebastian: That's right. Give it a try now. Are you ready? Hit this!

Alma: Oops! I completely missed it!

Sebastian: That's alright, try again.

Alma: Oh, I see. Let me try again...

Sebastian: Here comes another ball... Wow! You hit it over the fence! You're a very powerful lady.

Alma: Haha. I guess I need to practice more!

31. Vivere In California – Living In California

Jessica: fa proprio freddo stamani.

Tatiana: hai ragione. Stamattina presto ho dovuto togliere la brina dal parabrezza dell'auto.

Jessica: non avrei mai pensato che potesse fare così freddo ai primi di dicembre, specie in California.

Tatiana: lo so. Stamani, quando mi sono svegliato, c'erano 40 gradi Fahrenheit. Stavo gelando subito dopo essermi alzato. Tutto quel freddo non è stato sicuramente piacevole.

Jessica: Non riesco a ricordare quando è stata l'ultima volta che ha fatto questo freddo a dicembre.

Tatiana: come se non bastasse il freddo, questo pomeriggio pioverà!

Jessica: caspita! Pioverà nel pomeriggio?

Tatiana: Non solo questo pomeriggio, ma anche per tutta la settimana. Al meteo hanno detto che incomincerà a piovigginare poco prima di mezzogiorno, e poi pioverà più forte verso le quattro.

Jessica: Immagino che questa settimana il tempo non migliorerà?

Tatiana: probabilmente entro sabato ci sarà un po' di sole. Ma prima che esca il sole nel fine settimana ci sarà nebbia, vento e pioggia.

Jessica: Sono contento che piova anche se non mi piace poi così tanto. Quest'anno ci sono state poche piogge.

Tatiana: Sì, ricordo a malapena quando ha piovuto l'ultima volta. Bene, finché non ci sono tuoni o lampi, posso reggere.

Jessica: raramente ci sono in California.

Tatiana: Siamo molto fortunati che la California abbia una delle migliori condizioni meteorologiche in America.

Jessica: hai ragione, ci sono posti peggiori in cui potremmo vivere. Bene, la lezione sta iniziando, ci vediamo dopo.

Tatiana: a più tardi.

LIVING IN CALIFORNIA

Jessica: It is so chilly this morning.

Tatiana: It certainly is. Early this morning I had to spray my car's windshield because it was covered with frost.

Jessica: I never would have thought it could be this cold in early December, especially in California.

Tatiana: I know. The temperature was 40 degrees Fahrenheit when I woke up this morning. I was freezing as soon as I got out of bed. The cold weather was definitely not a nice surprise.

Jessica: I can't remember when it was actually this cold in December.

Tatiana: What's worse is that it's going to rain this afternoon. It's going to be cold and wet!

Jessica: Yuck! It's going to rain this afternoon?

Tatiana: Not just this afternoon, but also the entire rest of the week. The news said that it would start to drizzle just before noon, and then it would rain really hard by four o'clock.

Jessica: I'm guessing there's no sign of better weather this week?

Tatiana: There is a slim chance of sunshine by Saturday. However, it will be foggy, windy, and rainy before the sun comes out this weekend.

Jessica: I am glad that it rains even though I do not like rainy weather. We have a very dry season so far this year.

Tatiana: Yes, I can hardly remember when it rained last time. Well, as long as there is no thunder or lightning, I can stand it.

Jessica: We rarely have thunder or lightning in California.

Tatiana: We are very lucky that California has one of the best weather conditions in America.

Jessica: You are right, there are worse places we could be living. Alright, class is starting right now so I'll see you later.

Tatiana: See you later.

32. Cuocere Al Forno Qualcosa Di Buono – Baking Goodness

Claudia: mamma, cosa stai cucinando? Che buon profumo.

Signora Eva: sto preparando dei dolci. È la tua torta di carote preferita.

Claudia: sembra deliziosa e vedo anche dei muffin. Sei molto indaffarata, vero?

Signora Eva: Sì. Donovan domani deve portare qualcosa ad una festa di compleanno. Quindi, quei muffin sono solo per lui. Non mangiarli

Claudia: posso prendere almeno un pezzo di torta di carote? Lo voglio adesso.

Signora Eva: Puoi aspettare dopo cena?

Claudia: La torta mi sta chiamando: "Claudia, mangiami ... mangiami ..." No, non voglio aspettare. Posso, mamma?

Signora Eva: Ah ah ... Ok, va bene.

Claudia: Yum! Allora cosa c'è per cena stasera?

Signora Eva: Farò il roast beef e la vellutata ai funghi.

Claudia: È da tanto che non fai la vellutata ai funghi. Mamma, hai bisogno di aiuto?

Signora Eva: No, vai a fare i compiti e lasciami la cucina libera.

Claudia: Grazie, mamma. Chiamami quando la cena è pronta. Non voglio aspettare per l'arrosto di manzo, la vellutata ai funghi, la torta di carote e i muffin.

Signora Eva: I muffin sono per Donovan. Non toccarli!

Claudia: lo so, mamma. Sto scherzando.

BAKING GOODNESS

Claudia: Mom, what are you cooking? It smells so good.

Mrs. Eva: I am baking cakes. This is your favorite carrot cake.

Claudia: It looks scrumptious. And I see muffins some over there too. You have been busy, haven't you?

Mrs. Eva: Yes. Donovan has to take some to a birthday party tomorrow. So, those muffins are just for him. Don't eat them.

Claudia: Can I have a piece of carrot cake? I want to enjoy life right now.

Mrs. Eva: You don't want to wait until after dinner?

Claudia: The cake is calling my name, "Claudia, eat me... eat me..." No, I don't want to wait. Can I, mom?

Mrs. Eva: Ha ha... Ok, go ahead.

Claudia: Yum! So what's for dinner tonight?

Mrs. Eva: I will make roast beef and cream of mushroom soup.

Claudia: It has been a long time since you made cream of mushroom soup. Do you need any help, mom?

Mrs. Eva: No, go do your homework and leave the cooking to me.

Claudia: Thanks, mom. Call me whenever dinner is ready. I do not want to be late for roast beef, cream of mushroom soup, carrot cake and muffins.

Mrs. Eva: The muffins are for Donovan. Do not touch them!

Claudia: I know, mom. I'm just kidding.

33. Assistenza Telefonica – Help Over The Phone

Gigi: Grazie per aver chiamato il Sports Recreation Center. Come posso aiutarla?

Carlotta: Ho acquistato una cyclette dal vostro negozio un paio di mesi fa e sto avendo dei problemi. Ha smesso di funzionare e vorrei poterla riparare.

Gigi: la metto in contatto col servizio assistenza. Attenda un momento per favore.

Angela: Servizio assistenza, sono Angela. Come posso aiutarla?

Carlotta: L'anno scorso ho acquistato una cyclette dal centro Sport che necessita una riparazione.

Angela: Quale è il problema che riscontra?

Carlotta: Non so cosa sia successo, ma lo schermo del computer non si accende più, rimane nero.

Angela: Ha provato a premere il pulsante Start?

Carlotta: Sì, non si accende nulla.

Angela: qual è il modello di cyclette che ha acquistato?

Carlotta: è una Skull Crusher 420Z +, è quella con il cesto nella parte anteriore.

Angela: Posso mandarle un tecnico per sistemare il difetto. Il lavoro le costerà $ 5.000,00. Inoltre, ci saranno delle spese aggiuntive in caso si debba procedere a sostituire qualche pezzo. Per lei va bene?

Carlotta: È costoso. I costi di riparazione non sono coperti dalla garanzia?

Angela: quando ha acquistato la sua bici?

Carlotta: circa 3 mesi fa.

Angela: mi dispiace, ma la garanzia standard copre solo un mese. Quando l'ha comprata ha anche acquistato l'estensione della garanzia?

Carlotta: No, non l'ho fatto. C'è un altro modo oltre a pagare $ 5,000.00 per la riparazione?

Angela: ho paura di no.

Carlotta: peccato.

HELP OVER THE PHONE

Gigi: Thank you for calling Sports Recreation Center. How may I help you?

Carlotta: I purchased an exercise bike from your store a couple months ago, and I am having problems with it. It stopped working and I need to have it repaired.

Gigi: Let me connect you to the Service department. One moment please.

Angela: Service department, this is Angela. How can I help you?

Carlotta: I bought an exercise bike from Sports Center last year and it needs to be repaired.

Angela: What seems to be the problem?

Carlotta: I am not what happened, but the computer screen is black and doesn't turn on anymore.

Angela: Did you try to press the Start button?

Carlotta: Yes, and nothing turns on.

Angela: What is your bike model?

Carlotta: It is a Skull Crusher 420Z+, it's the one with the really cool basket in the front.

Angela: I can send a technician out to take a look at your bike. It will cost $5,000.00 for labor. Also, if we have to replace any parts, that will be extra. Sound like a deal?

Carlotta: That is expensive. Isn't the repair cost covered by warranty?

Angela: When did you purchase your bike?

Carlotta: About 3 months ago.

Angela: I am sorry. The standard warranty only covers 1 month. Did you buy extra warranty coverage at the time of purchase?

Carlotta: No, I did not. Are there any other options besides paying $5,000.00 for repair labor?

Angela: No, I am afraid not.

Carlotta: Damnit.

34. ANDIAMO AD UN CONCERTO – LET'S GO TO A CONCERT

Letizia: hei Natalia, Umberto, c'è un concerto al parco stasera con una gran bella scaletta. Volete andare?

Natalia: Io non lavoro stasera quindi posso sicuramente venire.

Umberto: Anche io, andiamo!

Natalia: C'è un bel traffico stasera ...

Umberto: Sì, perché il traffico è così congestionato?

Letizia: probabilmente perché la gente sta andando al parco per il concerto. È un'ottima band conosciuta e fa un'ottima musica.

Natalia: Sì, hai ragione. Negli ultimi quattro anni, non ho mai perso un loro concerti. Ogni volta che scopro che si esibiscono in città, compro subito il biglietto.

Umberto: da quando hanno iniziato a suonare qui?

Natalia: Hanno iniziato sei anni fa e ogni anno suonano per tutta la prima settimana di giugno.

Letizia: Umberto, questa sera ti divertirai. Ci sarà buona musica, tutti a ballare e sicuramente si urlerà parecchio. Potremmo anche ritrovarci in mezzo ad un mosh pit.

Umberto: Non vedo l'ora, sembra molto divertente.

Natalia: io preferisco la musica rap; ma devo dire che la musica country può essere piacevole. Strano ma vero, potrei ascoltarla per tutto il giorno.

Letizia: Umberto, che tipo di musica ti piace?

Umberto: Oh, mi piacciono tutti i generi musicali purché non sia musica aggressive.

Natalia: Wow, lo stadio è pieno di gente! Sono sorpresa da quanta gente c'è per il concerto. È stata un'ottima idea venire prima!

LET'S GO TO A CONCERT

Letizia: Hey Natalia, Umberto, there is a concert in the park tonight with a great line up. Do you want to go?

Natalia: I don't work tonight so I can definitely go.

Umberto: Me too, let's go!

Natalia: There's a ton of cars out tonight...

Umberto: Yea, why is the traffic so heavy?

Letizia: People are probably heading toward the park for the concert. It's a very popular band and they play really good music.

Natalia: Yes, they do. For the last four years, I have never missed one of their concerts. Every time I find out that the band is coming to town I buy a ticket right away.

Umberto: How long ago did the band start playing here locally?

Natalia: They started a tradition six years ago and now every year they play the whole first week of June.

Letizia: Umberto, you are really going to enjoy this evening. There will be good great music, a lot of jumping around, and definitely a lot of shouting. They may even have a mosh pit.

Umberto: I can't wait, it sounds like a lot fun.

Natalia: My favorite is gangster rap music; however, I have to say that country music can be pleasant to listen to. Surprisingly, I can listen to it all day long.

Letizia: Umberto, what kind of music do you like?

Umberto: Oh, I like all kinds of music as long as it is not aggressive.

Natalia: Wow, the stadium is packed with people! I'm surprised at the number of people who have already shown up for the concert. It's a good thing we're here already!

35. Organizzare – Making Plans

Alessia: Lisa, dimmi ... Quali sono i tuoi programmi per il fine settimana?

Lisa: non lo so. Vuoi fare qualcosa insieme?

Sara: ti piacerebbe vedere un film? AMC 24 su Parker Road sta dando: *Se mi lasci, ti cancello.*

Alessia: Volevo già vederlo! È come se mi leggessi nella mente. Vuoi prima andare a cena fuori?

Sara: Per me va bene. Dove vuoi che ci incontriamo?

Lisa: incontriamoci al Red Rooster House. È da un bel po' che ci vado.

Alessia: ancora un'ottima idea. Ho sentito dire che hanno aggiunto nel menu un nuovo primo. Dovrebbe essere buono perché la Red Rooster House ha sempre il miglior cibo italiano in città.

Sara: a che ora ci vediamo?

Lisa: Beh, il film lo proiettano alle 13:00, alle 14:00, alle 16:00 e alle 18:00.

Alessia: Perché non andiamo allo spettacolo delle 16:00? Possiamo incontrarci al Red Rooster House alle 13:00. Avremo tempo a sufficienza.

MAKING PLANS

Alessia: Lisa, tell me... What are your plans for this upcoming weekend?

Lisa: I don't know. Do you want to get together and do something?

Sara: How do you feel about going to see a movie? AMC 24 on Parker Road is showing *If You Leave Me, I Delete You.*

Alessia: I've been wanting to see that! It's like you read my mind. Do you want to go out to dinner beforehand?

Sara: That's fine with me. Where do you want to meet?

Lisa: Let's meet at the Red Rooster House. It's been a while since I've been there.

Alessia: Good idea again. I heard they just came out with a new pasta. It should be good because Red Rooster House always has the best Italian food in town.

Sara: When should we meet?

Lisa: Well, the movie is showing at 1:00PM, 2:00PM, 4:00PM and 6:00PM.

Alessia: Why don't we go to the 4:00PM show? We can meet at Red Rooster House at 1PM. That will give us enough time.

36. Vacanze Invernali – Winter Break

Amedeo: ehi Matteo, dai prendi i tuoi bagagli e sali.

Matteo: Va bene, Amedeo. Grazie per avermi dato un passaggio a casa. Di solito i miei genitori mi vengono a prendere, ma stasera lavorano fino a tardi.

Amedeo: Non preoccuparti, sono contento di poterti aiutare.

Matteo: A proposito, quando giocheremo di nuovo a basket?

Amedeo: sicuramente dopo la pausa invernale, c'è comunque da aspettare un bel pò. Farai qualcosa in queste vacanze?

Matteo: Non proprio. Oltre al basket, lavorerò soltanto.

Amedeo: lavori? Hai avuto un nuovo lavoro o lavori ancora al Twisters?

Matteo: Beh, Twisters è stato un buon primo lavoro e le persone erano davvero gentili. Ma, le mansioni erano molto impegnative ed era diventato difficile andare sia a scuola che lavorare.

Amedeo: capisco, cosa fai esattamente?

Matteo: lavoro in un call center, reparto tecnologia e vendite. All'inizio è stato un po' difficile, ma ora mi sono abituato a parlare al telefono con degli estranei.

Amedeo: ottimo. Quando hai iniziato?

Matteo: in Techmerica sto lavorando dal 1° ottobre. Hai organizzato qualcosa per le vacanze?

Amedeo: un viaggio ad Aspen con lo snowboard. Dovresti venire se non sei troppo impegnato col tuo nuovo lavoro.

Matteo: sarebbe fantastico! Grazie per l'invito.

Winter Break

Amedeo: Hey Matteo, if you're ready to go just throw your all of your stuff in the trunk and ride in the front seat.

Matteo: Alright, Amedeo. Thank you for giving me a ride home. Usually my parents pick me up, but they had to work late tonight.

Amedeo: No worries, I'm glad I could help.

Matteo: By the way, when is our next basketball game?

Amedeo: It is sometime after winter break, but anyways it's a long time from now. Have you made any plans for the break though?

Matteo: Not really. Other than going to basketball practice, I'll just be working.

Amedeo: Working? Did you get a new job or are you still working at Twisters?

Matteo: Well, Twisters was a good first job and the people were really great to work with. However, the schedule was very demanding which made it difficult to go to school and work.

Amedeo: Well, what are you doing now at your new job?

Matteo: I am working in technology sales. It's at a call center. It was a little difficult at first, but now I am used to talking to strangers on the phone.

Amedeo: Oh, that sounds great. When did you start the new job?

Matteo: I have been with Techmerica since October 1st. Do you have any plans for break?

Amedeo: I am planning a snowboarding trip to Aspen. You should come if you're not too busy at the new job.

Matteo: Oh, that sounds like fun! Thank you for the invitation.

37. Dal Medico – Visiting The Doctor

Dottore: Buon giorno, Cristina.

Cristina: Buon giorno, dottore.

Dottore: dalla sua cartella clinica, vedo che si è sentita stanca circa un mese fa, e poi ha iniziato ad avere l'emicrania. Ha anche avuto mal di stomaco e la febbre?

Cristina: No, dottore.

Dottore: mi permetta di visitarla.

Dottore: per favore faccia un respiro profondo, lo trattenga e poi espiri. Ancora una volta grazie.

Dottore: recentemente ha modificato la sua dieta vedendo qualche cambiamento di peso?

Cristina: Ho perso cinque kg di recente, ma non ho affatto cambiato la mia dieta.

Dottore: Per caso soffre di insonnia?

Cristina: quando vado a letto mi è difficile addormentarmi subito e spesso mi sveglio durante la notte.

Dottore: beve o fuma sigarette?

Cristina: No.

Dottore: sembra che lei abbia la polmonite. Oltre questo, non riscontro altre problematiche. Per il momento, deve riposare e fare un po' di attività fisica. Le prescrivo qualcosa per la polmonite. È allergica a qualche farmaco?

Cristina: No, che io sappia.

Dottore: Va bene. Prenda questo farmaco tre volte al giorno dopo aver mangiato.

Cristina: Grazie, dottore.

Dottore: a rivederLa.

VISITING THE DOCTOR

Doctor: Good morning, Cristina.

Cristina: Good morning, Doctor.

Doctor: Looking at your information, I see that you started feeling tired about a month ago, and then you started having migraines.

You have also had an upset stomach a fever also?

Cristina: No, doctor.

Doctor: Let me do a quick physical checkup.

Doctor: Please take a deep breath, hold your breath, and then exhale. One more time please.

Doctor: Have you made any changes to your diet or seen fluctuation in your weight recently?

Cristina: I lost five pounds recently, but I haven't changed my diet at all.

Doctor: By chance do you suffer from insomnia?

Cristina: It is difficult for me to fall asleep when I go to bed. I also wake up a lot during the night.

Doctor: Do you drink or smoke cigarettes?

Cristina: No.

Doctor: It appears that you have pneumonia. Besides that, I do not see any other problems. For now, get some rest and do some exercise.

I am going to give you a prescription for the pneumonia. Are you allergic to any medications?

Cristina: Not that I am aware of.

Doctor: Alright. Take this medication three times a day after you eat.

Cristina: Thank you, Doctor.

Doctor: You are welcome.

38. AL MERCATO – THE MARKET

Laura: Gioia, stamattina, prima di andare a lavoro, la mamma mi ha chiesto di fare la spesa. Solo che non posso andarci per via del mio progetto scolastico. Puoi andarci tu al posto mio?

Gioia: certo che posso, ho finito quello che dovevo fare. La mamma cosa ha detto di comprare?

Laura: Oltre al pollo, al pesce e alle verdure, possiamo comprare qualsiasi altra cosa che vogliamo per fare colazione o per gli spuntini. L'importante è che la spesa sia sufficiente per tutta la settimana.

Gioia: c'è qualcosa in particolare che vuoi per colazione?

Laura: la farina d'avena, come al solito.

Gioia: non voglio mangiare la farina d'avena tutti i giorni. Prenderò i pancake e lo sciroppo.

Laura: Se riesci a trovarli, prendi i nuovi pancake senza glutine nella sezione benessere, per favore. Voglio vedere se hanno un sapore diverso.

Gioia: c'è ancora abbastanza caffè e panna per mamma e papà?

Laura: Sì, la possiamo fare. In effetti, dovresti anche comprare il latte. È quasi finito.

Gioia: dai, cosa vuoi come spuntini?

Laura: le patatine vanno più che bene. Sicuramente tu vorrai i biscotti al cioccolato.

Gioia: conoscendomi è meglio che scriva tutte queste cose, altrimenti potrei dimenticarle fin tanto che arrivo al negozio. Non vorrei dover fare due viaggi!

THE MARKET

Laura: Gioia, before mom left for work this morning she asked me to go grocery shopping. The problem is that I need to finish my school project. Can you go for me?

Gioia: I am finished with my chores, so I can go to the store for you. What did mom want you to buy?

Laura: Besides chicken, fish and vegetables, we can buy whatever else we want for snacks and breakfast. She basically wanted me to buy enough groceries for the entire week.

Gioia: Is there anything specifically you want for breakfast?

Laura: I guess some oatmeal as usual.

Gioia: I don't want oatmeal every day. I will buy some pancakes and syrup then.

Laura: If you can find it, get the new gluten free pancakes in the health section please. I want to see if it tastes any different.

Gioia: Is there still enough coffee and cream for mom and dad?

Laura: Yes, we do. In fact, you should buy some milk also. We almost out of it.

Gioia: Next, what do you want for snacks?

Laura: Some chips would be fine with me. You probably want your chocolate cookies.

Gioia: Knowing myself it's probably better that I write all these things down or else I will forget them by the time I get to the market. I would hate to have to make two trips!

39. Prendere Un Appartamento – Let's Get An Apartment

Danilo: Ehi, Dario. Che ci fai qui?

Dario: Sto cercando un appartamento da affittare. Tu invece? Stai anche tu cercando un appartamento?

Danilo: Sì. La casa dei miei genitori è molto lontana, quindi mi piacerebbe trovare un appartamento più vicino a scuola e al lavoro.

Dario: Ok, capisco. Non ho ancora deciso se voglio una casa da condividere con altri o prendere un appartamento solo per me.

Danilo: Allora, cosa stai cercando?

Dario: Non ho bisogno di molto per essere onesto. Tutto ciò di cui ho bisogno è un posto abbastanza grande per mettere il mio letto e la mia scrivania. Certo, ho bisogno che ci sia una cucina in modo da poter cucinare e risparmiare così un po' di soldi.

Danilo: sembra proprio quello che sto cercando. Non posso lavorare a tempo pieno come ho fatto durante l'estate. Trascorrerò la maggior parte del mio tempo a studiare e per questo non potrò lavorare molto. Tutto ciò di cui ho bisogno è un posto che sia sicuro, silenzioso e pulito.

Dario: L'altro problema è che non posso pagare per un intero appartamento. La maggior parte dei posti che ho visto sono abbastanza costosi.

Danilo: hai pensato di condividere un appartamento con qualcuno? Se vuoi, possiamo trovare un appartamento con due camere da letto e viverci insieme. Potrebbe essere una soluzione più economica.

Dario: Questo potrebbe risolvere il nostro problema. Proviamo?

Danilo: Sì, potrebbe essere un'ottima idea. Andiamo a vedere se ci piace questo appartamento.

LET'S GET AN APARTMENT

Danilo: Hey, Dario. What are you doing here?

Dario: I am looking for an apartment to rent. What are you doing here? Are you looking for an apartment also?

Danilo: Yes. My parents' house is really far away so I'd like to find an apartment that is closer to school and my job.

Dario: Ok, that makes sense. I still haven't decided if I want to stay in the dorms or get my own apartment.

Danilo: So, what are you looking for?

Dario: I don't need much to be honest. All I need is a place big enough for my bed and desk. Of course, it needs to have a kitchen so that I can cook my meals and save a little bit of money.

Danilo: That sounds like what I'm looking for too. I can't work full-time like I did during the summer. I will be spending most of my time studying so I won't be able to work as much. All I need is something safe, quiet and clean.

Dario: The other issue is paying for an entire apartment for myself. Most places I have seen are very expensive.

Danilo: Have you thought about sharing an apartment? If you want, we can find a two-bedroom apartment and share it. It may be cheaper that way.

Dario: That could solve our problem. Do you want to try it?

Danilo: Yes, that could be a great idea. Let's go check this one out and see if we like it.

40. Il Chiosco – The Concession Stand

Simone: C'è un chiosco lì. Volete qualcosa?

Daniela: No niente, grazie. Ho già la mia bottiglia d'acqua.

Chiara: io voglio un sacchetto di patatine e una birra fredda. Sei sicuro di non volere un hot dog, Daniela?

Daniela: si, mia madre sta arrostendo delle bistecche per cena, e non voglio mangiare troppo qui.

Chiara: Daniela, sei così fortunata ad avere un'ottima cuoca per madre. Simone, uno di questi giorni devi assolutamente assaggiare la sua torta ai mirtilli. Sinceramente, in città non ho mai assaggiato nulla di simile.

Daniela: In effetti, stasera mia madre sta preparando la sua torta di mirtilli! Simone, se ti va, ti metto un pezzo da parte.

Simone: certo mi piacerebbe assaggiarla.

Daniela: E tu, Chiara? Un pezzo di torta anche per te?

Simone: Chiara, farai meglio a prendere subito le patatine e la birra, se li vuoi ancora. Sono quasi le 15:00 e lo spettacolo sta per iniziare.

Chiara: ultima possibilità. Siete sicuri di non voler niente?

Daniela: Sono sicura, grazie Chiara.

Simone: anch'io, Chiara.

Chiara: Ok, tenetemi il posto, torno subito.

THE CONCESSION STAND

Simone: There is a food stand over there. Do you two want anything?

Daniela: Nothing for me, thanks. I already have my bottle of water.

Chiara: I want a bag of chips and a cold beer. Are you sure you do not want a hot dog, Daniela?

Daniela: I am quite sure. My mom is cooking a good steak dinner, and I want to make sure I don't eat too much here.

Chiara: Daniela, you are so lucky to have such a good cook for a mother. Simone, you have to taste her blueberry pie one of these days. Honestly, there's no better pie in this whole town.

Daniela: In fact, my mom is baking her blueberry pie tonight! I you would like, I will save you a piece, Simone.

Simone: Don't tease me with a good time! I would love that.

Daniela: How about you, Chiara? A piece of cake for you too?

Simone: Chiara, you better get your snacks and beer now if you still want them. It is almost 3:00PM, and the show is about to start.

Chiara: Last chance to get something. Are you guys sure you don't want anything?

Daniela: I am sure, thank you Chiara.

Simone: Me neither, Chiara.

Chiara: Ok, save my seat and I will be right back.

41. Ora Di Pranzo – Lunchtime

Emilia: Tiziana, dopo pranzo posso chiamare la mamma col tuo cellulare?

Tiziana: certo, Emilia. Non dimenticarti di salutarmela.

Maira: Emilia, potresti passarmi il pepe, per favore?

Emilia: Certamente, ecco qua.

Maira: E anche il sale, per favore. Grazie.

Emilia: di nulla.

Tiziana: ti dispiacerebbe se ci fermassimo al Strand Bookstore per prendere un film?

Emilia: No, per niente.

Maira: Ho sentito che hanno dei nuovi libri e mi piacerebbe fermarmi per dare un'occhiata.

Tiziana: ho ordinato troppo cibo. Qualcuno vuole favorire?

Emilia: Sì, io. Sembra delizioso.

Tiziana: E tu, Maira?

Maira: No, grazie. Ho già abbastanza cibo.

Emilia: Tiziana, ti piacerebbe assaggiare una delle mie fajitas?

Tiziana: Sì, grazie.

Emilia: tieni. Ne vuoi un'altra?

Tiziana: Oh, no questa è più che sufficiente! Grazie.

Maira: abbiamo finito tutte di mangiare? Dovremmo partire ora per evitare il traffico; altrimenti faremo tardi.

Tiziana: io sono pronta, appena lo siete anche voi partiamo.

Emilia: Anch'io sono pronta. Andiamo.

LUNCHTIME

Emilia: Tiziana, May I borrow your cell phone to call my mother after lunch?

Tiziana: Yes, of course, Emilia. Don't forget to tell her we said hello.

Maira: Emilia, could you pass the pepper, please?

Emilia: Certainly, here you are.

Maira: And the salt too, please. Thank you.

Emilia: You're welcome.

Tiziana: Would either of you mind if we stop by Strand Bookstore on the way to the movie?

Emilia: No, not at all.

Maira: I heard they have a new book selection so I would love to stop by and check it out.

Tiziana: I ordered too much food. Would anybody care to try some of my food?

Emilia: Yes, I would like some. It looks delicious.

Tiziana: How about you, Maira?

Maira: No, thank you. I have enough food already.

Emilia: Tiziana, would you like to taste one of my fajitas?

Tiziana: Yes, please.

Emilia: Here you go. Do you want another?

Tiziana: Oh, that is more than enough! Thank you.

Maira: I imagine we are all finished eating? We should leave now to avoid the traffic; otherwise we will be late.

Tiziana: I am ready to leave whenever you all are.

Emilia: So am I. Let's go.

42. CERCANDO LAVORO – SEARCHING FOR A JOB

Matilda: Ciao Paolo, che bello rivederti.

Paolo: anche per me, Matilda. È passato molto tempo dall'ultima volta che ci siamo visti.

Matilda: Sì, l'ultima volta che ci siamo visti è stato intorno ad Halloween. Come stai?

Paolo: Sto bene. Potrebbe andare meglio se trovassi un nuovo lavoro.

Matilda: Perché ne stai cercando uno nuovo?

Paolo: Beh, mi sono diplomato la scorsa settimana. Ora, vorrei trovare un lavoro nel campo finanziario.

Matilda: è da tanto che lo stai cercando?

Paolo: ho iniziato questa settimana

Matilda: hai preparato il curriculum, giusto?

Paolo: Sì.

Matilda: non mi preoccuperei allora. Sei molto ambizioso e so che investirai tutte le tue energie per ottenere ciò che desideri. Poi devi considerare che questo è un buon periodo per trovare lavoro, tutte le società hanno bisogno di un analista finanziario.

Paolo: lo spero. Grazie per il consiglio.

SEARCHING FOR A JOB

Matilda: Hi Paolo, it is good to see you.

Paolo: Same here, Matilda. It has been a long time since I last saw you.

Matilda: Yes, the last time we saw each other was around Halloween. How is everything?

Paolo: I am doing OK. It would be better if I had a new job.

Matilda: Why are looking for a new job?

Paolo: Well, I graduated last week. Now, I want to get a job in the Finance field.

Matilda: Have you been looking for a new job for a while?

Paolo: I just started this week.

Matilda: You have prepared a resume, right?

Paolo: Yes.

Matilda: I wouldn't worry then. You have a lot of ambition and I know you will put all of your energy into getting what you want. Besides, the job market is really good right now, and all companies need financial analysts.

Paolo: I hope so. Thank you for the advice.

43. Colloquio Di Lavoro – Job Interview

Mario: Benvenuto Pietro. Iniziamo il colloquio. È pronto?

Pietro: Sì, lo sono.

Mario: fantastico. Prima di tutto, lasci che mi presenti. Sono il direttore della logistica aziendale. Ho bisogno di coprire una posizione entry-level il prima possibile.

Pietro: meraviglioso. Potrebbe parlarmi della posizione e delle sue aspettative?

Mario: il nuovo dipendente dovrà lavorare a stretto contatto con il reparto di produzione. C'è anche l'obbligo di trattare giornalmente con la banca.

Pietro: Che tipo di qualifiche richiede?

Mario: è richiesta una laurea quadriennale in economia aziendale. Sarebbe utile avere avuto qualche esperienza pregressa.

Pietro: Che tipo di esperienza sta cercando?

Mario: aver fatto un lavoro d'ufficio. Non è necessario avere molta esperienza, chi otterrà il lavoro potrà farsela sul posto di lavoro.

Pietro: È fantastico!

Mario: quali sono i suoi pregi? Perché dovrei assumerla?

Pietro: Sono una persona che lavora sodo e che impara velocemente. Non vedo l'ora di poter imparare e soprattutto vado d'accordo con tutti.

Mario: Va bene. Non le dispiace lavorare per molte ore, vero?

Pietro: No, non mi dispiace affatto.

Mario: sa gestire la pressione?

Pietro: Sì. Quando andavo a scuola, seguivo cinque corsi al semestre e in più lavoravo almeno venticinque ore a settimana.

Mario: Ha qualche domanda da fare?

Pietro: No, penso di avere capito bene le future mansioni.

Mario: Ok, Pietro è stato bello conoscerla. Grazie per essere venuto al colloquio.

Pietro: Piacere di averla conosciuta. La ringrazio di tutto.

Job Interview

Mario: Welcome Pietro. Let's start the interview. Are you ready?

Pietro: Yes, I am.

Mario: Great. First of all, let me properly introduce myself. I am the company Logistics Manager. I need to fill an entry-level position as soon as possible.

Pietro: Wonderful. Could you tell me a little bit about the position and your expectations?

Mario: The new employee will have to work closely with the manufacturing department. There is also a requirement to deal with the bank on a daily basis.

Pietro: What type of qualifications do you require?

Mario: I require a four-year college degree in business administration. Some previous work experience would be helpful.

Pietro: What kind of experience are you looking for?

Mario: General office work is fine. I do not require a lot of experience. There will be on the job training for the right person.

Pietro: That is great!

Mario: What are your strengths? Why should I hire you?

Pietro: I am a hard-working person and a fast learner. I am very eager to learn, and I get along fine with everyone.

Mario: Alright. You do not mind working long hours, do you?

Pietro: No, I do not mind at all.

Mario: Can you handle pressure?

Pietro: Yes. When I was going to school, I took 5 courses each semester while working at least twenty-five hours every week.

Mario: Do you have any questions for me at this time?

Pietro: No, I think I have a pretty good understanding of the job.

Mario: Ok, Pietro it was nice meeting you. Thank you for coming.

Pietro: Nice meeting you too. Thank you for seeing me.

44. Fare Una Presentazione – Giving A Presentation

Emma: venerdì dovrò fare una presentazione sul riscaldamento globale e sono molto nervoso.

Olga: ci sono molte cose che puoi fare per allentare il nervosismo ed essere più sicuro di te.

Emma: cosa dovrei fare, Olga?

Olga: hai fatto delle ricerche sull'argomento?

Emma: certo, ho fatto molte ricerche sull'argomento, e so che posso rispondere a quasi tutte le domande che il pubblico potrebbe farmi.

Olga: fatti una scaletta dei punti da argomentare.

Emma: hai ragione. Questo mi aiuterà a organizzare tutte le informazioni.

Olga: Sì. Ti aiuterà a capire quale argomento trattare all'inizio e così via...

Olga: è un'ottima idea per rendere credibile la tua presentazione! È importante che tu abbia degli argomenti per la tua presentazione.

Emma: la faccio adesso! Grazie.

Olga: farai un'ottima presentazione.

Giving A Presentation

Emma: I will have to give a presentation on global warming on Friday, and I am so nervous.

Olga: There are a lot of things you can do to make you feel more confident and less nervous.

Emma: What should I do, Olga?

Olga: Have you done your research on the topic?

Emma: In fact, I have done a lot of research on the subject, and I know I can answer almost any questions I will receive from the audience.

Olga: Make sure to create an outline of your presentation.

Emma: You're right. This will help me organize all of the information.

Olga: Yes. It will help you figure out what should present first, second, third…

Olga: Good idea! It is important to have facts to support your presentation. You want the presentation to be credible.

Emma: I'm going to do that right now! Thank you.

Olga: You're going to have a great presentation.

45. La Laurea – Graduation

Lisa: che meraviglioso mazzo di fiori. Per chi è?

Anna: Questi fiori sono per mia sorella Silvia. Oggi si laurea.

Lisa: li avrai pagati molto.

Anna: Li ho pagati settanta dollari.

Lisa: piuttosto cari.

Anna: Mia sorella, negli ultimi quattro anni, ha studiato molto per raggiungere questo traguardo. Valgono tutti i soldi che ho speso.

Lisa: È molto gentile da parte tua. Vorrei che ci stessimo laureando anche noi oggi. Sarebbe fantastico!

Anna: ci rimangono solo altri tre anni. Ci troveremo alla laurea senza neppure rendercene conto. Il tempo passa molto velocemente.

GRADUATION

Lisa: That is a wonderful bouquet of flowers. Who is it for?

Anna: These flowers are for my sister Silvia. She is graduating today.

Lisa: It must have cost you a fortune.

Anna: I paid seventy dollars for them.

Lisa: That is quite expensive.

Anna: My sister worked very the last four years for her degree. To me spending that amount of money is worth it.

Lisa: That is very nice of you. I wish we were graduating today. This is so exciting!

Anna: We only have another three years and we will be done also. We'll be graduating before we realize it. Time goes by very fast.

46. Halloween – Halloween

Mario: Roberta, ma ci pensi che domani è già Halloween? Il tempo passa così in fretta! Oggi è il 30 ottobre! Hai già deciso quale costume mettere?

Roberta: Sono ancora indecisa. Non so se mettere il costume da tostapane o quello da rapper. Mi sono sempre chiesta perché sia una tradizione travestirsi ad Halloween.

Mario: travestirsi rende molto più divertente festeggiarlo!

Roberta: Sì, ricordo che mi sono divertita un sacco l'anno scorso quando mamma mi ha portato in giro travestita da gatto. Tu, Mario, sai già come travestirti?

Mario: voglio un costume da scoiattolo!

Roberta: è una bella idea!

Mario: fantastica! Quindi tu sarai un rapper ed io uno scoiattolo. Andiamo a chiedere a mamma se domani sera, possiamo andare in giro da soli per il "dolcetto o scherzetto".

Roberta: Ok, andiamo!

HALLOWEEN

Mario: Can you believe that tomorrow is Halloween Roberta? Time goes by so fast! Today is October 30th! Have you already decided what costume you want to wear?

Roberta: I'm still undecided. I want to wear either a toaster costume or a gangster rapper costume. I have always wondered why it's a tradition to dress up for Halloween.

Mario: Dressing up makes celebrating the holiday much more fun!

Roberta: Yes, I remember having a lot of fun last year when mom took me around in a cat outfit. Do you know what you want to be yet, Mario?

Mario: I want to be a chipmunk!

Roberta: That's a great idea!

Mario: Great! So you will be a gangster rapper and I will be a chipmunk. Let's go ask mom if we can go trick-or-treating tomorrow night by ourselves.

Roberta: Ok, let's go ask mom!

47. Ad Un Hotel – At A Hotel

Personale dell'hotel: buonasera.

Francesco: Buonasera. Gentilmente, io e mia moglie stiamo cercando una stanza per la notte. Per caso ne ha una disponibile?

Personale dell'hotel: avete prenotato?

Francesco: Purtroppo, non abbiamo fatto la prenotazione.

Personale dell'hotel: d'accordo. Mi faccia controllare se c'è qualche stanza disponibile. È fortunato. Ne è rimasta una.

Francesco: perfetto. Abbiamo guidato tutto il giorno e siamo molto stanchi. Abbiamo solo bisogno di un posto dove poterci rilassare per il resto della notte.

Personale dell'hotel: questa stanza dovrebbe andare bene allora. Si tratta di una camera con letto matrimoniale molto comoda e completa di cucina.

Francesco: qual è il suo costo a notte?

Personale dell'hotel: viene 179 $. Oltre voi due pernotterà qualcun'altro?

Francesco: siamo solo noi due. So che è già tardi a quest'ora, ma c'è qualche ristorante aperto nelle vicinanze?

Personale dell'hotel: C'è un ristorante nell'hotel che rimarrà aperto per un'altra ora. Vuole pagare la stanza con carta di credito?

Francesco: Sì. Tenga.

Personale dell'hotel: la ringrazio. Ecco a lei, vi auguro un buon pernottamento.

At a Hotel

Hotel Receptionist: Good evening.

Francesco: Hello, good evening. My wife and I need a room for the night please. By chance do you have one available?

Hotel Receptionist: Do you have a reservation?

Francesco: Unfortunately, we do not have a reservation.

Hotel Receptionist: Ok. Let me check and see what we have. It looks you're in luck. We have only one room left.

Francesco: Excellent. We have been driving all day and we're very tired. We just need a place to relax for the rest of the night.

Hotel Receptionist: This room should do just fine then. It is a cozy room with a king size bed and full kitchen.

Francesco: How much is it for the night?

Hotel Receptionist: It's $179 for the room. Is there anyone else staying in the room with you?

Francesco: It's just the two of us. I know that it's late at night, but is there any restaurant open nearby?

Hotel Receptionist: There's a restaurant open for another hour in the hotel. Do you want to pay for the room with a credit card?

Francesco: Yes. Here you go.

Hotel Receptionist: Thank you. You're all set. Enjoy the rest of the night.

48. Uno Studente Straniero – A Foreign Student

Raimondo: Salve, lei è la signora Elena?

Signora Elena: Sì, sono io. Tu devi essere Raimondo. Ti stavo aspettando.

Raimondo: Dovevo arrivare due giorni fa, ma il mio volo dalla Colombia è stato ritardato.

Signora Elena: Beh, l'importante è che tu abbia viaggiato sicuro. Gradisci un tè?

Raimondo: si ne prendo un po', se non è troppo il disturbo. Ha una bella casa.

Signora Elena: Grazie. Cinque anni fa, dalla Colombia ci siamo trasferiti in California e abbiamo deciso di acquistare questa casa. Ci piace molto.

Raimondo: Le ho portato un regalo.

Signora Elena: Oh, non avresti dovuto. è una bella collana. Grazie. Per quanto tempo starai qui?

Raimondo: di nulla. Ho intenzione di rimanere in California per cinque mesi per imparare bene l'inglese. Sono davvero entusiasta di andare a scuola per impararlo.

Signora Elena: ottimo, lascia che ti mostri la tua stanza, così puoi metterti comodo. Sarai stanco dopo tutto quel viaggio.

A FOREIGN STUDENT

Raimondo: Hello, are you Mrs. Elena?

Mrs. Elena: Yes, I am. You must be Raimondo. We have been expecting you.

Raimondo: I was supposed to arrive two days ago, but my flight out of Colombia was delayed.

Mrs. Elena: Well, I'm glad that you made it safely, that's is what is most important. Would you like some tea?

Raimondo: I would love some, if it's not too much trouble. You have a beautiful home.

Mrs. Elena: Thank you. We moved to California from Colombia five years ago and decided to buy this house. We absolutely love it.

Raimondo: I brought you a gift.

Mrs. Elena: Oh, you shouldn't have. This is a beautiful necklace. Thank you. How long will you be here for?

Raimondo: You're welcome. I plan to stay in California for five months to practice speaking English. I am really excited to go to the English school and learn.

Mrs. Elena: Well, let me show you your room and you can relax. You must be tired from all of the traveling.

49. PROCRASTINARE – PROCRASTINATION

Renzo: hai già scritto la tua relazione? Dovrà essere pronta entro due settimane.

Marta: No, non l'ho ancora iniziata. Ho molto tempo ancora, sicuramente inizierò la prossima settimana.

Renzo: Ricordo che è quello che hai detto la scorsa settimana e la settimana prima. Visto che hai così tanto tempo libero durante le vacanze, dovresti farla in questo periodo.

Marta: Il problema è che sto facendo fatica in quella classe e penso di aver bisogno di un tutor. Altrimenti c'è la probabilità che non riesca a farla.

Renzo: ho una soluzione. Smetti di pensare e cercati un tutor.

Marta: hai ragione. Devo attivarmi e cercarne uno. Lo farò domani.

Renzo: domani? No, devi trovarne uno oggi!

Marta: Lo so, sto solo scherzando. Lo farò oggi.

PROCRASTINATION

Renzo: Have you written your research report yet? It's due in two weeks.

Marta: No, I haven't started working on it yet. I have plenty of time to do it next week though.

Renzo: I distinctly remember that's what you said last week and the week before that. Since you have so much free time during the holiday you should get it done.

Marta: The problem is that I am struggling in that class and I think I might need to get a tutor. Otherwise I might fail the entire class.

Renzo: I have a solution. Stop thinking about getting help and get a tutor.

Marta: You're right. I need to be proactive and get help. I start looking tomorrow.

Renzo: Tomorrow? No, you have to find one today!

Marta: I know, I'm just kidding. I will do it today.

50. Dove È Mio Fratello – Where's My Brother

Clarissa: Non riesco a trovare mio fratellino, Daniele. Pensavo che fosse proprio dietro di me e invece è scomparso. Mi aiuti per favore.

Poliziotto: probabilmente si è perso tra la folla. Ci sono molte persone che fanno compere per le vacanze. Che tipo di vestiti indossa?

Clarissa: ha una giacca blu e pantaloncini neri. Ha solo 5 anni.

Poliziotto: penso di averlo visto entrare nel camerino. Mi faccia controllare. Ha i capelli biondi?

Clarissa: Sì. L'ha trovato?

Poliziotto: No, non è lui. Controlliamo accanto, nel negozio di giocattoli.

Clarissa: Ama giocare con i Lego, avrei dovuto pensarci prima!

Poliziotto: vedo molti bambini. Qualcuno di loro è suo fratello?

Clarissa: Daniele! Eccoti qua, non l'ho fare mai più! Mi hai fatto preoccupare!

Poliziotto: tienilo d'occhio in modo che non accada più. lasciarlo girovagare da solo può essere pericoloso.

Clarissa: Ha ragione. Starò più attento.

Poliziotto: Va bene. Ora vada a cercare i suoi genitori, buona giornata.

Clarissa: la ringrazio agente per il suo aiuto.

WHERE'S MY BROTHER

Clarissa: I can't find my little brother, Daniel. I thought he was right behind me and now he's missing. Please help me.

Police officer: He probably got lost in the crowd. There are a lot of people shopping for the holidays. What kind of clothes is he wearing?

Clarissa: He has a blue jacket and black shorts. He's only 5 years old.

Police officer: I think I saw him go into the dressing room. Let me check. Does he have blonde hair?

Clarissa: Yes. Did you find him?

Police officer: No, that was not him. Let's check the toy store next door.

Clarissa: He loves playing with Legos, I should have thought of that!

Police officer: I see a lot of children everywhere. Are any of them your brother?

Clarissa: Daniel! There you are, don't you wander off like that again! You scared me to death!

Police officer: Please keep an eye on him so that this doesn't happen again. It can be dangerous wandering around all by himself.

Clarissa: You're right. I will take better care of watching him.

Police officer: Alright. Now go find your parents and have a good day.

Clarissa: Thank you officer for all of your help.

CONCLUSION

Well reader, we hope that you found these dual language dialogues helpful. Remember that the best way to learn this material is through repetition, memorization and conversation.

We encourage you to review the dialogues again, find a friend and practice your Italian by role playing. Not only will you have more fun doing it this way, but you will find that you will remember even more!

Keep in mind, that every day you practice, the closer you will get to speaking fluently.

You can expect many more books from us, so keep your eyes peeled. Thank you again for reading our book and we look forward to seeing you again.

ABOUT THE AUTHOR

Touri is an innovative language education brand that is disrupting the way we learn languages. Touri has a mission to make sure language learning is not just easier but engaging and a ton of fun.

Besides the excellent books that they create, Touri also has an active website, which offers live fun and immersive 1-on-1 online language lessons with native instructors at nearly anytime of the day.

Additionally, Touri provides the best tips to improving your memory retention, confidence while speaking and fast track your progress on your journey to fluency.

Check out https://touri.co for more information.

Want the Next Italian Book for Free?

https://touri.co/premium-access-italian-dialogues/

ONE LAST THING...

If you enjoyed this book or found it useful, we would be very grateful if you posted a short review on Amazon.

Your support really does make a difference and we read all the reviews personally. Your feedback will make this book even better.

Thanks again for your support!

Made in the USA
Monee, IL
07 February 2022

90893233R00085